Contents

Introduction

There are many loop CDs on the market filled with drum loops and samples. If you're not a great drum programmer, sampling a drum loop is a great way to get a groove going so that you can begin writing a song. However, there isn't a lot of material out there for non-keyboard players, or even keyboardists who want a harmonic foundation for their songs. Many young musicians struggle with voicings and try to "match" chords in a pattern, but they are unable to "grab" the chords they hear. In this book, all the grooves are transcribed, so you can fully understand the content of the music you're working with.

The Dictionary of Keyboard Grooves CD is filled with keyboard patterns that can be sampled and looped in a groove. The audio and MIDI files can be edited with respect to tempo, key, and sound, then used to create songs or play-along tracks. They are also useful as learning tools for knowledge of voicing and style. These loops will be a formidable addition to your MIDI production and a great writing tool.

How to Use the CD
Sampling

On the audio portion of this multimedia CD, each loop has a track number. The loop can be sampled directly into your sampler. Just run the line out of your CD player into your sampler, check the level, then record and follow procedures set by the manufacturer to save and loop the sample. For use in your sequencer, go to the file menu, then import, open, or load samples from the CD into the sequencer and save to the local hard drive. The samples are stored in folders according to style, and the loops are individually numbered.

If you are using your sampler to record these loops, be careful not to distort the input level. Listening while you record is the easiest way to know if you're overloading the signal. On the other hand, be sure to get a "hot" enough signal so that you don't have to turn up the gain later. A signal around 0 to –3 dB is safe. The record level meter should peak somewhere in the middle. Of course, you may be able to edit the volume once it is recorded, depending on your gear and its capabilities; but a good, even recording level is always the best place to start.

Music Programs

For use with music programs on a computer, the loops can be loaded directly from the CD into the sequencer audio track. The loops can then be customized in audio editor software such as Acid, Sound Forge, Wavelab, and many others. These programs can edit pitch and tempo, cut and paste, add effects, and much more.

MIDI Files

The Dictionary of Keyboard Grooves CD also contains MIDI files. Again, you can import these into any sequencer. The advantage to this is the powerful editing capabilities. The musical content is there, but the sound can be routed into your own MIDI gear. The tempo, key, octave, and any other MIDI function can be implemented. Once the data is saved as a song in your sequencer, you may print out the score. The index numbers for the loops will match the MIDI file tracks for easy referencing.

Dictionary of

Keyboard Grooves

by GAIL JOHNSON

Dedicated to Paula, my inspiration and vein, my Groove Master!

Thank You:

John Baker, my engineer
Aaron "Vane" Jones, my groove inspiration
Tamina, my new musician

ISBN 978-0-634-01878-7

7777 W. BLUEMOUND RD. P.O. BOX 13819 MILWAUKEE, WI 53213

Visit Hal Leonard Online at
www.halleonard.com

Chapter One

1

DANCE GROOVES

Including Disco, House, and Party Song Material using Synth Instrumentation

Groove #	Style	BPM	Key
101	Very Fast	120	G
102	Very Fast	120	A
103	Very Fast	120	A$\flat$
104	Very Fast	120	A$\flat$
105	Fast	109	E$\flat$mi
106	Fast	109	E$\flat$mi
107	Slow	80	C
108	Very Fast	120	Ami
109	Fast	105	B$\flat$
110	Very Fast	122	Ami
111	Fast	105	F
112	Very Fast	122	Gmi
113	Very Fast	122	B$\flat$
114	Fast	118	Ami
115	Fast	118	E$\flat$mi
116	Very Fast	120	Fmi
117	Very Fast	120	Emi
118	Very Fast	120	Cmi
119	Fast	109	Gmi
120	Fast	110	Ami

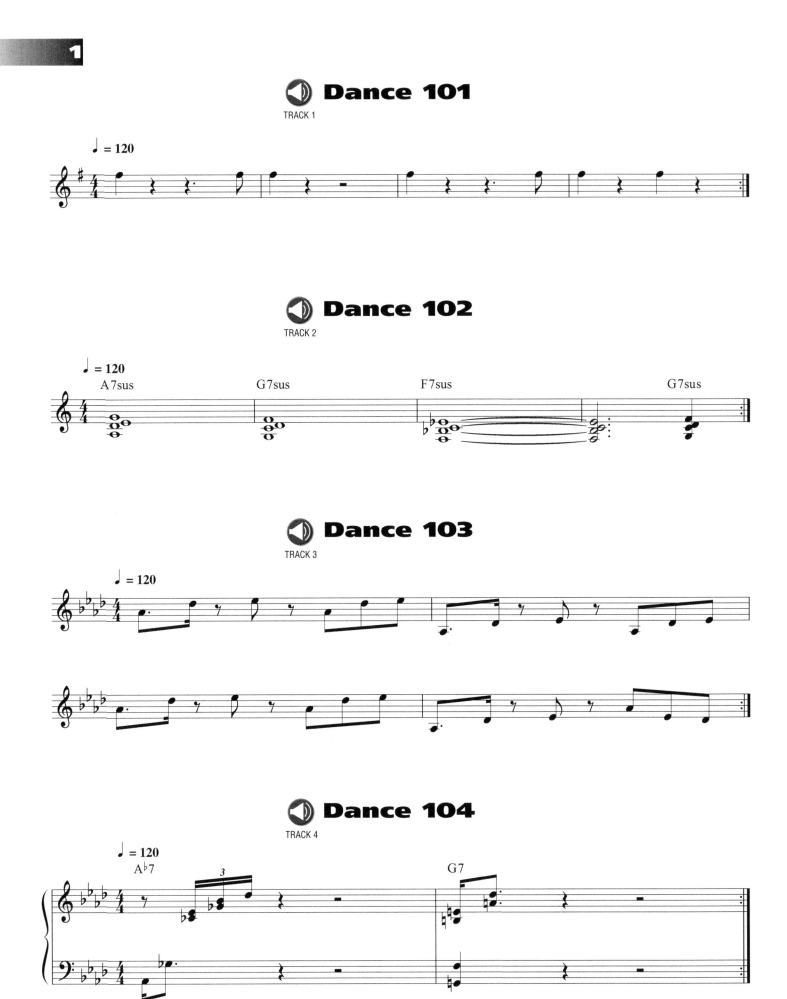

Dance 105
TRACK 5

Dance 106
TRACK 6

Dance 107
TRACK 7

Dance 108
TRACK 8

Dance 109

TRACK 9

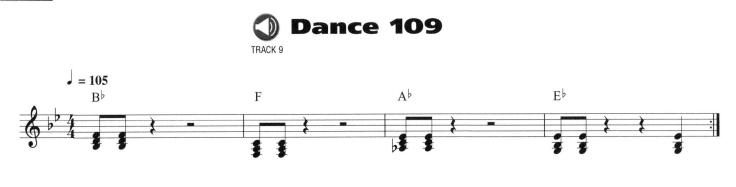

Dance 110

TRACK 10

Dance 111

TRACK 11

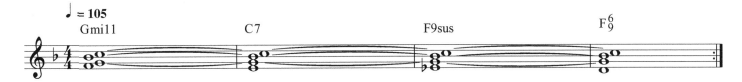

Dance 112

TRACK 12

Dance 113

TRACK 13

Dance 114

TRACK 14

Dance 115

TRACK 15

Dance 116

TRACK 16

Dance 117

TRACK 17

Dance 118

TRACK 18

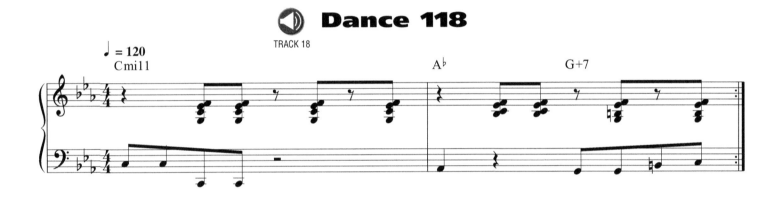

Dance 119

TRACK 19

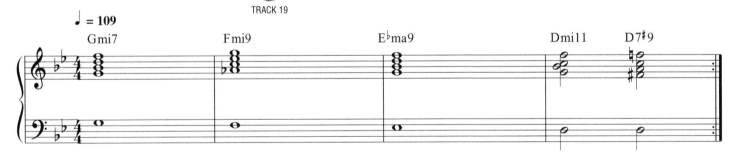

Dance 120

TRACK 20

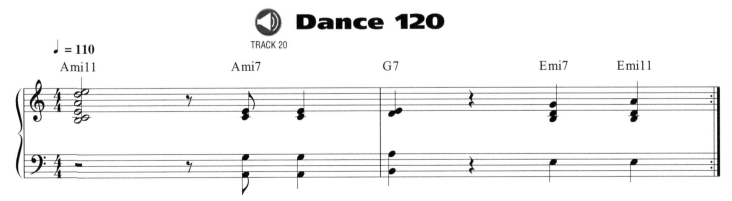

Chapter Two

2 FUNK GROOVES

Including Clavinet, Dirty Rhodes, Organ, and Synth

Some of the grooves included here are taken from this author's *Funk Keyboards* book/CD.

Groove #	Style	BPM	Key
201	Fast	110	E Phrygian
202	Fast	110	E♭mi
203	Fast	110	Dmi
204	Mid-Tempo	95	B♭
205	Mid-Tempo	100	C
206	Mid-Tempo	90	Bmi
207	Mid-Tempo	105	C
208	Very Fast	144	B♭
209	Fast	108	Emi
210	Mid-Tempo	90	Gmi
211	Fast	118	A♭
212	Fast	118	F♯mi
213	Fast	118	C
214	Fast	110	Ami
215	Fast	110	Ami
216	Fast	110	Ami

Funk 201

TRACK 21

$\quad = 110$

E7sus

Funk 202

TRACK 22

$\quad = 110$

E♭mi7 — A♭7

E♭mi7 — A♭7

Funk 203

TRACK 23

$\quad = 110$

Dmi7 — G7

Dmi7 — G7

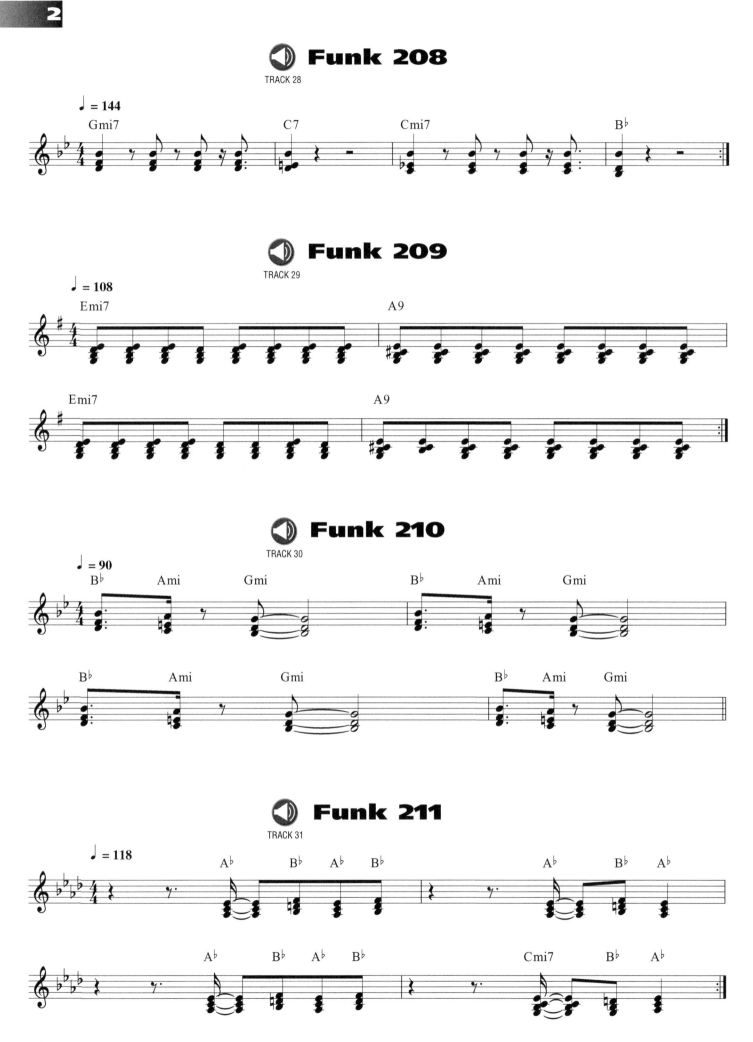

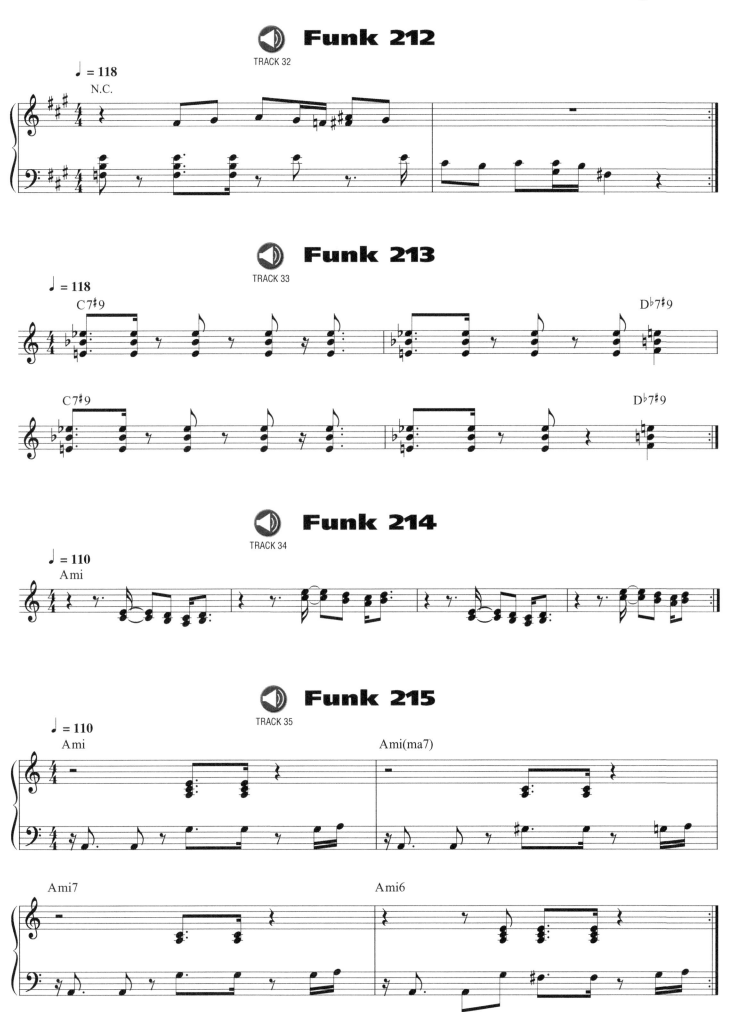

Funk 212

TRACK 32

Funk 213

TRACK 33

Funk 214

TRACK 34

Funk 215

TRACK 35

Funk 216

TRACK 36

Chapter Three

3

JAZZ GROOVES

Standard Progressions and Turnarounds for Piano and Organ

Groove #	Style	BPM	Key
301	Fast	110	D
302	Slow	75	Dmi
303	Very Fast	130	C
304	Fast	100	B♭
305	Mid-Tempo	95	E♭
306	Mid-Tempo	95	Dmi
307	Moderately Slow	80	B
308	Moderately Slow	80	B♭
309	Slow	70	Cmi
310	Slow	80	E♭
311	Fast	100	Ami

Jazz 301

TRACK 37

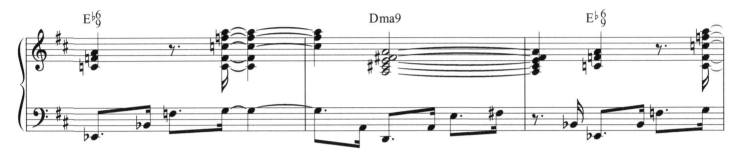

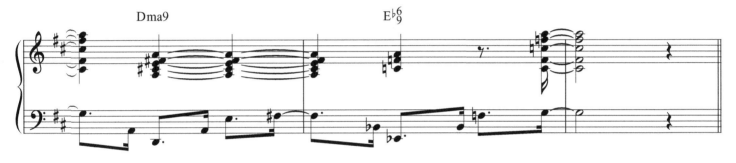

Jazz 302

TRACK 38

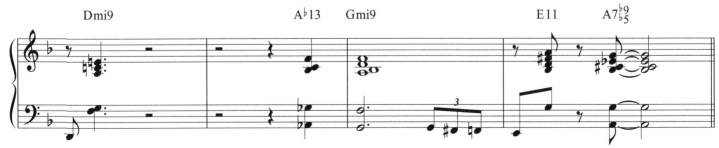

Jazz 303

TRACK 39

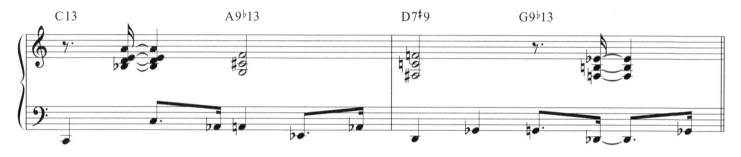

Jazz 304

TRACK 40

Jazz 305

TRACK 41

Jazz 305

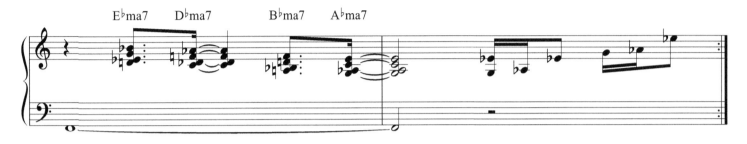

Jazz 306

TRACK 42

Jazz 307

TRACK 43

Jazz 308

TRACK 44

Jazz 309

TRACK 45

Jazz 310

TRACK 46

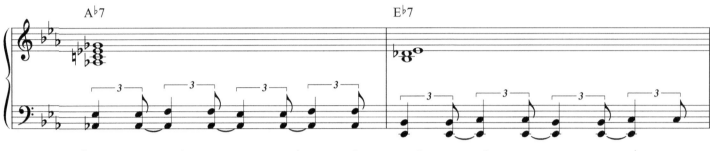

Jazz 311

TRACK 47

Chapter Four

4 LATIN GROOVES

Montunos, Cha-Chas, and Various Patterns for Piano

Groove #	Style	BPM	Key
401	Very Fast	120	Cmi
402	Fast	110	Bmi
403	Very Fast	117	Ami
404	Mid-Tempo	105	Ami
405	Mid-Tempo	90	Cmi
406	Mid-Tempo	95	Gmi
407	Mid-Tempo	90	F
408	Mid-Tempo	90	F
409	Very Fast	120	Dmi
410	Very Fast	120	G
411	Very Fast	120	A♭mi
412	Very Fast	125	E♭mi
413	Moderately Slow	80	Fmi
414	Moderately Slow	80	B♭
415	Fast	110	Dmi

Latin 403

TRACK 50

Latin 404

TRACK 51

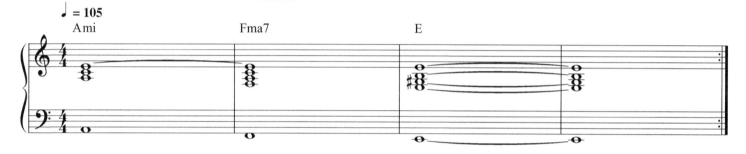

Latin 405

TRACK 52

Latin 406

TRACK 53

Latin 407

TRACK 54

Latin 408

TRACK 55

Latin 409

TRACK 56

Latin 410

TRACK 57

Latin 411

TRACK 58

Latin 412

TRACK 59

Latin 413

TRACK 60

Latin 414

TRACK 61

Chapter Five

5 REGGAE GROOVES

Various Upbeat Grooves: Organ, Marimba, and Clavinet

Groove #	Style	BPM	Key
501	Mid-Tempo	80	F
502	Very Fast	125	C
503	Very Fast	125	E♭mi
504	Very Fast	130	C♯mi
505	Very Fast	125	Cmi
506	Mid-Tempo	80	Ami
507	Mid-Tempo	80	Dmi
508			
509	Mid-Tempo	85	C
510	Mid-Tempo	85	F
511	Fast	110	Fmi

Reggae 501

TRACK 62

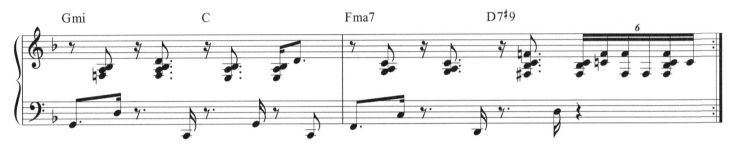

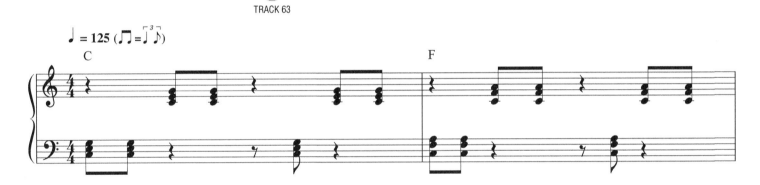

Reggae 502

TRACK 63

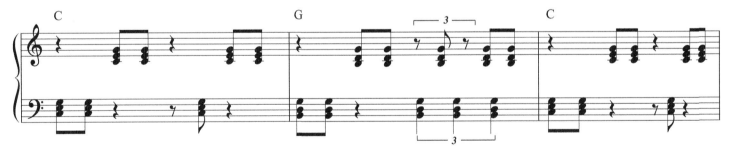

Reggae 503

TRACK 64

Reggae 504

TRACK 65

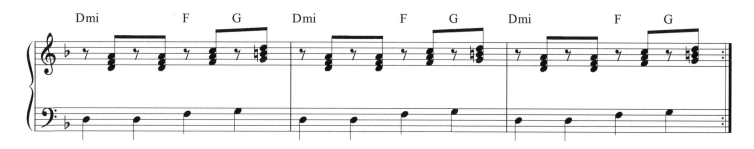

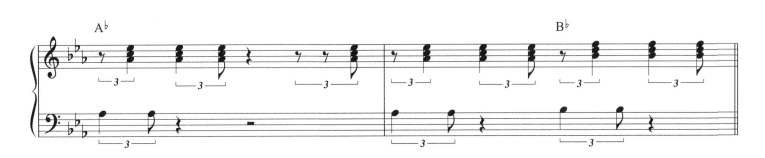

Reggae 505

TRACK 66

Reggae 506

TRACK 67

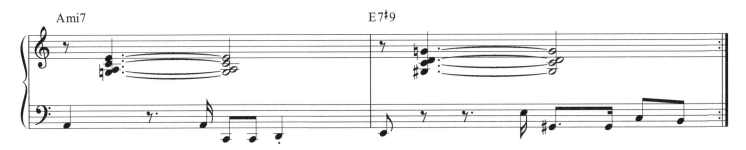

Reggae 507

TRACK 68

Reggae 508

TRACK 69

Reggae 509

TRACK 70

Reggae 510

TRACK 71

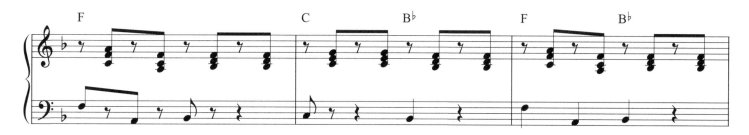

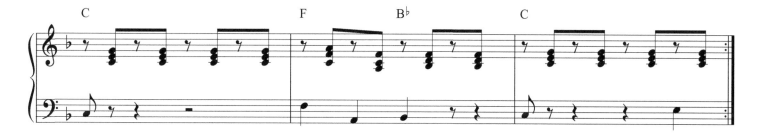

Reggae 511

TRACK 72

♩ = 110

Chapter Six

6

R&B BALLADS

Standard Patterns Using Rhodes, Strings, Bells, and Pads

Some of these slow ballads are also used frequently in "smooth jazz." These can be very sultry and mood-setting.

Groove #	Style	BPM	Key
601	Moderately Slow	75	Emi
602	Slow	70	C
603	Slow	70	B♭ mi
604	Slow	70	Bmi
605	Very Slow	60	D♭
606	Fast	100	C
607	Moderately Slow	75	F
608	Mid-Tempo	80	Fmi
609	Moderately Slow	75	F Lydian
610	Moderately Slow	75	C
611	Slow	60	F Lydian
612	Mid-Tempo	85	C
613	Slow	60	D
614	Moderately Slow	75	Fmi

R&B 601

TRACK 73

R&B 602

TRACK 74

R&B 603

TRACK 75

R&B 604

TRACK 76

R&B 605

TRACK 77

R&B 606

TRACK 78

R&B 607

TRACK 79

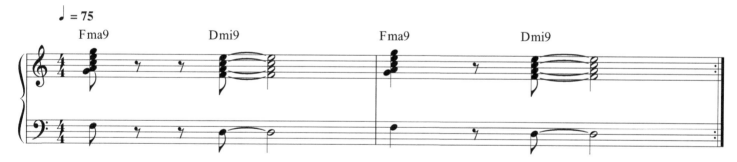

R&B 608

TRACK 80

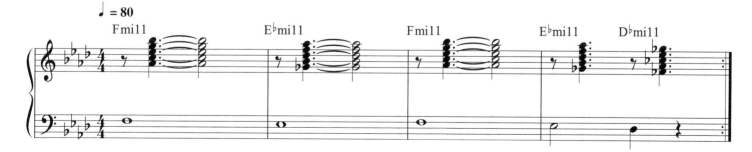

TRACK 81

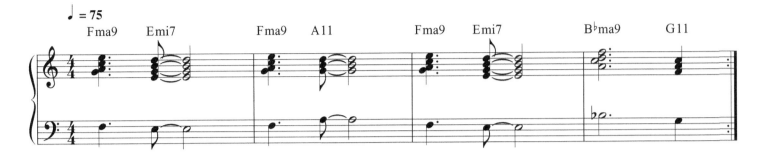

TRACK 82

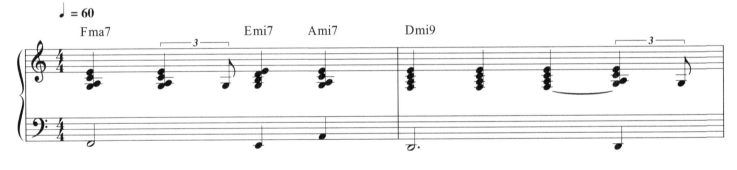

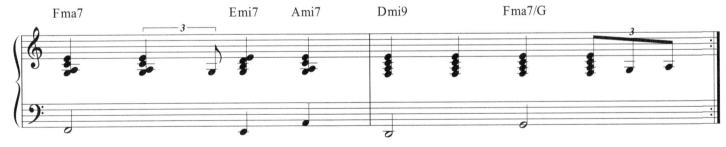

R&B 612

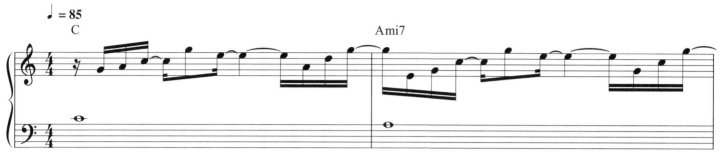

R&B 613

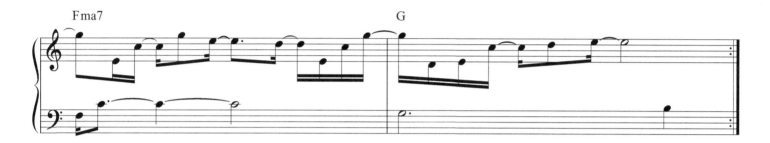

R&B 614

Chapter Seven

ROCK 'N' ROLL PIANO

Licks Popularized by Little Richard, Fats Domino, and Jerry Lee Lewis

These patterns, mostly on piano, use "power chords," and the tempos can get very fast; you'll need a lot of muscle to keep up!

Groove #	Style	BPM	Key
701	Fast	115	C
702	Very Fast	125	C
703	Slow	70	Fmi
704	Slow	70	F
705	Very Fast	140	A♭
706	Fast	100	G
707	Very Fast	120	G
708	Fast	100	G
709	Fast	115	C
710	Very Fast	145	G
711	Very Fast	170	G

R&R 701

TRACK 87

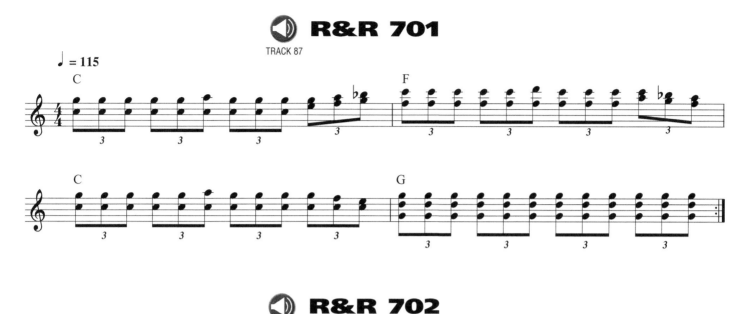

R&R 702

TRACK 88

R&R 703

TRACK 89

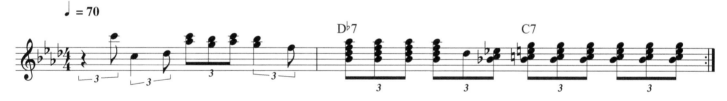

R&R 704

TRACK 90

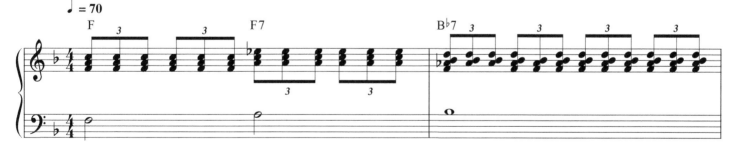

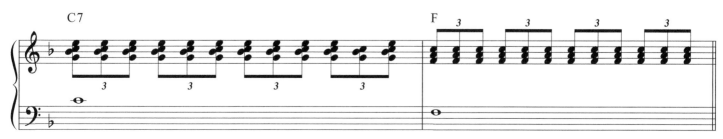

R&R 705

TRACK 91

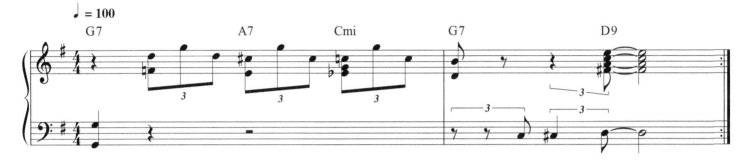

R&R 706

TRACK 92

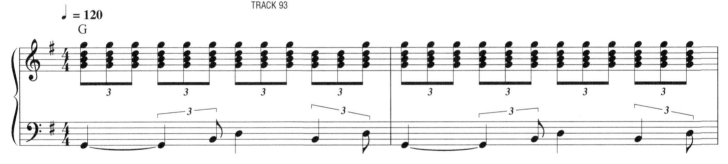

R&R 707

TRACK 93

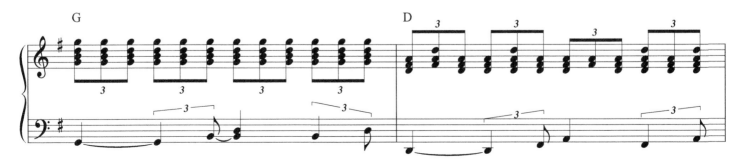

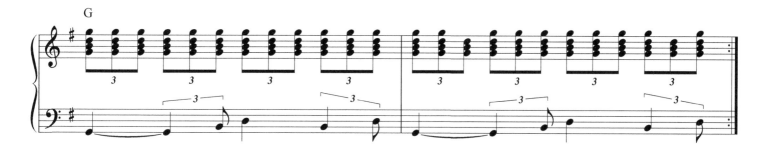

R&R 708

TRACK 94

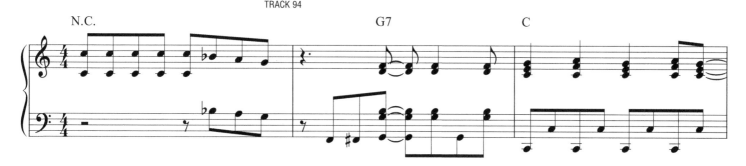

R&R 709

TRACK 95

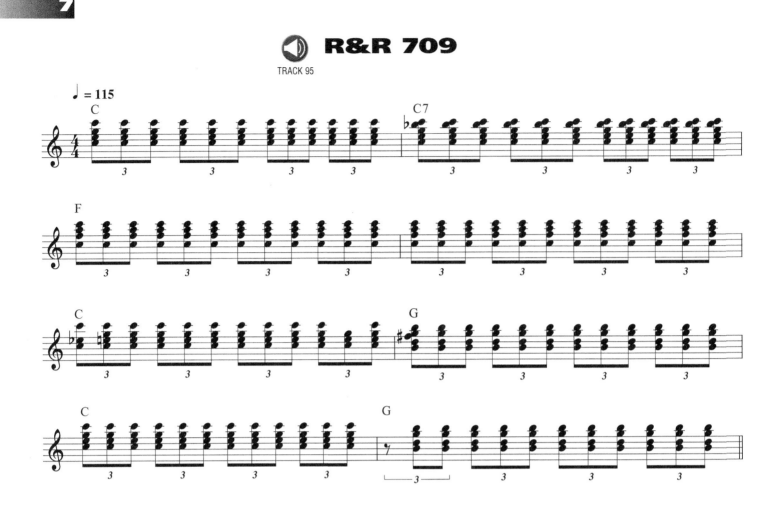

R&R 710

TRACK 96

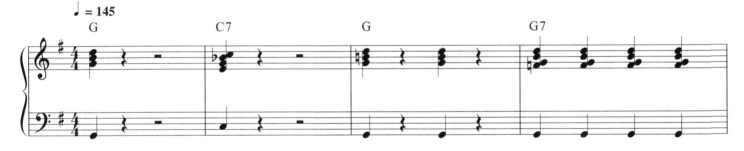

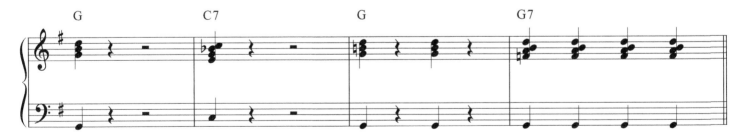

R&R 711

TRACK 97

About the Author

Born and raised in Philadelphia, PA, Gail Johnson began playing piano at age 10. Having earned a degree in composition from the Berklee College of Music, she currently splits her time between her staff position at Musicians Institute and her music director position with Norman Brown/Warner Brothers Records. In addition to a busy schedule of songwriting, producing, piano instruction, and occasional TV appearances, she also finds time to accompany the youth choir and band.

Gail has toured and recorded with Pink, Minako Honda, The Newtrons, Jermaine Jackson, Morris Day, Bobby Womack, Ray Parker Jr., Vesta, Howard Hewitt (Shalamar), and was music director for Milli Vanilli.

Her various television performances include "BET on Jazz," "Lou Rawls / Parade of Stars," "Soul Train," "The Arsenio Hall Show," and "Solid Gold." In the realm of contemporary jazz, Gail has shared the stage with Bobby Lyle, Phil Perry, Kevin Toney, J. Spencer, O.C. Smith, Cal Bennett, Norman Brown, and Karen Briggs. She has also played for the theater productions *Eubie, the Eubie Blake Story,* and the Langston Hughes play *Tambourines to Glory,* and was songwriter and music director for the gospels *Saving Grace* and *Reason for the Season,* written by Dennis Rowe.

Presently, this mother of two accompanies and records the Rainbow Choir (a children's gospel choir), gives piano instruction to elementary school children, transcribes music charts, and produces songs for many talented young artists. She has recently written the Hal Leonard MI Press book *Funk Keyboards: a Contemporary Guide to Chords, Rhythms, and Licks* (HL00695336).

Gail is a Kurzweil, Mackie, and SKB endorsee.

Musicians Institute Press

is the official series of Southern California's renowned music school, Musicians Institute. **MI** instructors, some of the finest musicians in the world, share their vast knowledge and experience with you – no matter what your current level. For guitar, bass, drums, vocals, and keyboards, **MI Press** offers the finest music curriculum for higher learning through a variety of series:

ESSENTIAL CONCEPTS
Designed from MI core curriculum programs.

MASTER CLASS
Designed from MI elective courses.

PRIVATE LESSONS
Tackle a variety of topics "one-on-one" with MI faculty instructors.

KEYBOARD

Funk Keyboards – The Complete Method
A Contemporary Guide to Chords, Rhythms, and Licks
by Gail Johnson • **Master Class**
00695336 Book/CD Pack $14.95

Jazz Hanon
by Peter Deneff • **Private Lessons**
00695554 . . . . $12.95

Keyboard Technique
by Steve Weingard • **Essential Concepts**
00695365 . . . . $12.95

Keyboard Voicings: The Complete Guide
by Kevin King • **Essential Concepts**
00695209 . . . . $12.95

Music Reading for Keyboard
by Larry Steelman • **Essential Concepts**
00695205 . . . . $12.95

R&B Soul Keyboards
by Henry J. Brewer • **Private Lessons**
00695327 Book/CD Pack $16.95

Salsa Hanon
by Peter Deneff • **Private Lessons**
00695226 . . . . $12.95

DRUM

Afro-Cuban Coordination for Drumset
by Maria Martinez • **Private Lessons**
00695328 Book/CD Pack $14.95

Blues Drumming
By Ed Roscetti • **Essential Concepts**
00695623 Book/CD Pack $14.95

Brazilian Coordination for Drumset
by Maria Martinez • **Master Class**
00695284 Book/CD Pack $14.95

Chart Reading Workbook for Drummers
by Bobby Gabriele • **Private Lessons**
00695129 Book/CD Pack $14.95

Drummer's Guide to Odd Meters
by Ed Roscehi • **Essential Concepts**
00695349 Book/CD Pack $14.95

Latin Soloing for Drumset
by Phil Maturano • **Private Lessons**
00695287 Book/CD Pack $14.95

Working the Inner Clock for Drumset
by Phil Maturano • **Private Lessons**
00695127 Book/CD Pack $16.95

VOICE

Harmony Vocals: The Essential Guide
by Mike Campbell & Tracee Lewis • **Private Lessons**
00695262 Book/CD Pack $17.95

Sightsinging
by Mike Campbell • **Essential Concepts**
00695195 . . . . $17.95

Vocal Technique
By Dena Murray • **Master Class**
00695427 Book/CD Pack $19.95

ALL INSTRUMENTS

An Approach to Jazz Improvisation
by Dave Pozzi • **Private Lessons**
00695135 Book/CD Pack $17.95

Encyclopedia of Reading Rhythms
by Gary Hess • **Private Lessons**
00695145 . . . . $19.95

Going Pro
by Kenny Kerner • **Private Lessons**
00695322 . . . . $17.95

Home Recording Basics Featuring Dallan Beck
00695655 Video $19.95

Harmony & Theory
by Keith Wyatt & Carl Schroeder • **Essential Concepts**
00695161 . . . . $17.95

Lead Sheet Bible
by Robin Randall • **Private Lessons**
00695130 Book/CD Pack $19.95

WORKSHOP SERIES

Transcribed scores of the greatest songs ever!

Blues Workshop
00695137 . . . . $22.95

Classic Rock Workshop
00695136 . . . . $19.95

Press

Musicians Institute Press

is the official series of Southern California's renowned music school, Musicians Institute. **MI** instructors, some of the finest musicians in the world, share their vast knowledge and experience with you – no matter what your current level. For guitar, bass, drums, vocals, and keyboards, **MI Press** offers the finest music curriculum for higher learning through a variety of series:

ESSENTIAL CONCEPTS
Designed from MI core curriculum programs.

MASTER CLASS
Designed from MI elective courses.

PRIVATE LESSONS
Tackle a variety of topics "one-on-one" with MI faculty instructors.

BASS

Arpeggios for Bass
by Dave Keif • **Private Lessons**
00695133 . . . . $12.95

The Art of Walking Bass
A Method for Acoustic or Electric Bass
by Bob Magnusson • **Master Class**
00695168 Book/CD Pack. $17.95

Bass Fretboard Basics
by Paul Farnen • **Essential Concepts**
00695201 . . . . $12.95

Bass Playing Techniques
by Alexis Sklarevski • **Essential Concepts**
00695207 . . . . $16.95

Grooves for Electric Bass
by David Keif • **Private Lessons**
00695265 Book/CD Pack. $14.95

Latin Bass
The Essential Guide to Afro-Cuban and Brazilian Styles
by George Lopez and David Keif •
Private Lessons
00695543 Book/CD Pack. $14.95

Music Reading for Bass
by Wendy Wrehovcsik • **Essential Concepts**
00695203 . . . . $10.95

Odd-Meter Bassics
by Dino Monoxelos • **Private Lessons**
00695170 Book/CD Pack. $14.95

GUITAR

Advanced Scale Concepts & Licks for Guitar
by Jean Marc Belkadi • **Private Lessons**
00695298 Book/CD Pack $14.95

Advanced Guitar Soloing
By Daniel Gilbert & Beth Marlis • **Essential Concepts**
00695636 Book/CD Pack. $19.95

Basic Blues Guitar
by Steve Trovato • **Private Lessons**
00695180 Book/CD Pack $14.95

Classical & Fingerstyle Guitar Techniques
by David Oakes • **Master Class**
00695171 Book/CD Pack. $14.95

Contemporary Acoustic Guitar
by Eric Paschal & Steve Trovato • **Master Class**
00695320 Book/CD Pack. $16.95

Creative Chord Shapes
by Jamie Findlay • **Private Lessons**
00695172 Book/CD Pack. $9.95

Diminished Scale for Guitar
by Jean Marc Belkadi • **Private Lessons**
00695227 Book/CD Pack. $9.95

Essential Rhythm Guitar
Patterns, Progressions and Techniques for All Styles
by Steve Trovato • **Private Lessons**
00695181 Book/CD Pack. $14.95

Funk Guitar: The Essential Guide
by Ross Bolton • **Private Lessons**
00695419 Book/CD Pack. $14.95

Guitar Basics
by Bruce Buckingham • **Private Lessons**
00695134 Book/CD Pack. $16.95

Guitar Hanon
by Peter Deneff • **Private Lessons**
00695321 . . . . $9.95

Guitar Lick-tionary
By Dave HIll • **Private Lessons**
00695482 Book/CD Pack. $17.95

Guitar Soloing
by Dan Gilbert & Beth Marlis • **Essential Concepts**
00695190 Book/CD Pack. $19.95
00695638 Video $19.95

Harmonics for Guitar
by Jamie Findlay • **Private Lessons**
00695169 Book/CD Pack. $9.95

Jazz Guitar Chord System
by Scott Henderson • **Private Lessons**
00695291 . . . . $7.95

Jazz Guitar Improvisation
by Sid Jacobs • **Master Class**
00695128 Book/CD Pack. $17.95
00695639 Video $19.95

Jazz-Rock Triad Improvising
by Jean Marc Belkadi • **Private Lessons**
00695361 Book/CD Pack. $14.95

Latin Guitar
The Essential Guide to Brazilian and Afro-Cuban Rhythms
by Bruce Buckingham • **Master Class**
00695379 Book/CD Pack. $14.95

Modern Approach to Jazz, Rock & Fusion Guitar
by Jean Marc Belkadi • **Private Lessons**
00695143 Book/CD Pack. $14.95

Modes for Guitar
by Tom Kolb • **Private Lessons**
00695555 Book/CD Pack. $16.95

Music Reading for Guitar
by David Oakes • **Essential Concepts**
00695192 . . . . $16.95

The Musician's Guide to Recording Acoustic Guitar
by Dallan Beck • **Private Lessons**
00695505 Book/CD Pack. $12.95

Practice Trax for Guitar
by Danny Gill • **Private Lessons**
00695601 Book/CD Pack. $14.95

Rhythm Guitar
by Bruce Buckingham & Eric Paschal •
Essential Concepts
00695188 Book. $16.95
00695644 Video $19.95

Rock Lead Basics
by Nick Nolan & Danny Gill • **Master Class**
00695144 Book/CD Pack. $15.95
00695637 Video $19.95

Rock Lead Performance
by Nick Nolan & Danny Gill • **Master Class**
00695278 Book/CD Pack. $16.95

Rock Lead Techniques
by Nick Nolan & Danny Gill • **Master Class**
00695146 Book/CD Pack. $15.95

Slap & Pop Technique For Guitar
00695645 Book/CD Pack. $12.95

Texas Blues Guitar
by Robert Calva • **Private Lessons**
00695340 Book/CD Pack. $16.95

FOR MORE INFORMATION, SEE YOUR LOCAL MUSIC DEALER, OR WRITE TO:

HAL•LEONARD® CORPORATION
7777 W. BLUEMOUND RD. P.O. BOX 13819 MILWAUKEE, WI 53213

Visit Hal Leonard Online at **www.halleonard.com**